Smilingwords

Charulatha Jain

Presentation by *BookLeaf Publishing*

Web: www.bookleafpub.com

E-mail: info@bookleafpub.com

ISBN: 9789358739923

First edition 2023

DEDICATION

This book is dedicated to my adorable parents: Maa, Smt. Sunitha Jain and Papa, Shri. Bachhraj Jain, in heaven. They have been my inspiration and this book is one of the many forms of gratitude to my dear parents. They personified freedom and independence and nurtured their three daughters, I being the youngest, with unconditional love, care and affection. They lived with broad-mindedness and openness just not by words but also by their actions.

Table of Contents

Birth	1
Childhood	2
The child chasing the school	3
Temples of Education	5
Sisters	6
Friends	7
Dreams	8
Travel Memory Lane	9
Nieces - The Princess	10
Melancholy Travel	12
First German Taste	13
Romanian Friend	14
Maa and Papa's Love	15
Maa ~ Mother	16
The Story of the Lone White Hibiscus	18
Marigold	19
Life is Beautiful	21
Privilege	22
I love to admit	23
Sweet Bitter Twenty-Five	24
Papa ~ Father	26

ACKNOWLEDGEMENT

I am deeply grateful to my sisters Swaati and Rashmi for believing in me and being a great support in my life journey. Friends have been an integral part of my life. My dear friends Shanmathi, Vishnu Ram, Vishnu CD, Namrata, Sneha, Sruthi V V and Mukundan listened to my poetic ramblings, offered valuable feedback and provided endless encouragement. I am grateful to my teacher Ms. Jayanthi Pateeswaran, who agreed to write the Foreword for this book without any second thoughts. My work is incomplete and biggest thanks to my nieces Sara and Tiah, who inspire me to connect with the inner child in me. My heartfelt gratitude goes to the publishers, designers, editors and the team who have helped turn my words and my emotions into reality.

I'm indebted to Mr. Sudhanshu Mani, the railway engineer who was the visionary behind Vande Bharat trains, for the blurb that captures the essence of my book

FOREWORD

Ms. Charulatha Jain is well known to me as she was my student at Shri Nehru Vidyalaya Higher Secondary School, Coimbatore, India. I had been associated with her closely as her English teacher. It has been a great pleasure guiding students like Charulatha as she used to be very responsible, responsive and a hard worker who takes criticism in the right sense. Even as a school student, she had a good command of the English language and could express herself flawlessly. So, it is not a surprise that her book with 21 poems will definitely prove her expertise. Not all of us are gifted with the talent to compose poetry.

Each poem has a personal touch. Childhood memories, joy, sorrow, love, affection, regard, respect, etc., all these emotions can be felt while reading the poems. The poem "I love to admit" expresses the admittance of her various feelings towards life and herself. "Sweet Bitter Twenty-Five" pays tribute to her parents and the part they had played in shaping her. I'm immensely proud of her achievements and wish Charulatha all success in her writing endeavors.

Birth

When the calendar was blooming
September was closer to ending
Mother was excited
Grandmother was impatient
A new beautiful soul was about to arrive

The hospital doors did signal
When Father entered the trail
Opening the doors at the hospital
Oxygen was consumed in additional

Painful Tears rolled on one end
Smiling Tears rolled on the other end
She was born
He was not born
The hearts were torn

Father had joy
Mother got the toy
Her sisters were overjoyed
She was the third
Adorable like the first and second
Charming in their world

Childhood

Innocence in her eyes
Fragrance of care & love in her mind
Negativity like eyes to the blind
Exciting games to play and find

Hopscotch to jump around picking stones
Ladders to climb around escaping snakes
Some of these games
Both teaching to focus on
What to avoid and what to pick
Are these tricks?

Mom's saree to hold on
Dad's hard hand to hold on
Bringing the comfort on
Patches of unknowns and fear
Childhood looked like a rapid-fire round

The child chasing the school

The morning hustle and bustle
The clock ticks chasing the home
As we shower and play with the foam
In queue to get the wavy hair comb

Fresh food in monochrome steel boxes
Arrive at school in the noon
everyone's favourite
Hot food under the hood

Building temples with sand
Building castles with sand
Building homes with sand
the mud particles in hand

Waiting for Dad while
Library and playground
Became the best friends
Rose mints, ice creams were the spends

School life is fun
Summer vacation calls for train
Cotton City to Cultural City
Luggage was always heavy

The innocent mind
Sisters playing cards
Window seats were on guard
Were the only battles played hard

Little did she wonder
Along with her sisters
She grew tall
She flew high
Attitude became taller and stronger positively
Dreams flew in clouds vividly
Making steps towards reality

Temples of Education

Draped in a violet saree
Under the shades of a tree
Did this girl know what she would become?
None could predict the future.

Circles, Equations, Formulas on the one hand
Handball, Volleyball on the other hand
She stayed away from the music band
All she admired was a stage with mic stand

Fourteen years she went on the bike
Dad always dropped her with the smile
Mom packed food with love
Teachers' pet was she

Stepping stones to success for future
Hand holding and shoulder lending for present
Teachers navigated the journey to sharpness from
blunt
Unleashed her skills like a treasure hunt

Schools and colleges played their roles
Seeds were being sown
regularly frequently
watered adequately
with friends and trips

Sisters

Playing lego blocks
Playing hide and seek
Sharing candies
Sharing beds

Mornings to Nights
We did fight as much as we
showered love and protection

Dad did business
and we played business

You are the reason I was there
You are the reason I still smile
Because we fight filled with love
Fuelled with endless care

Treasuring that moment
Reliving that moment
When I write this
I know I own the space
in your hearts forever

Friends

My filter coffee moment
The hot burst
Talking emotions out
That was a moment
Much needed coffee moment

Where you can have deep conversations
Where you can have meaningful conversations
Where you can smile
Where you can trust
Where you would greet cheers with Pizza
Where you celebrate friendship.
May be with chips
May be with trips
But sure of grips
For that unbreakable bond
Where one is just fond
of each other

Dreams

I stand alone yet surrounded
I dance alone in my thoughts
Look at my branches they are bare but strong with
scars
Look at the clouds behind
Look at the mist around
Look around green lush
Does that give me a push
I stand still yet with a will
to grow to glow
Dreams that show
Dreams that I breathe
Dreams that I live
Dreams that are like a beehive
Help me reach sky high

Travel Memory Lane

I stand there smiling
My sister was clicking
That rainy day
Let me say
That messy hair
Life is fair
Little did I know
My Travel flow
Would erupt
Would disrupt

5 years down the lane
When Google photo tells me the dates
Reminding me of those moments
Making me smile again
Hoping to travel again

Nieces - The Princess

This was on click three
When the pink rose
On the background
Hit the right chords

Holding a just-born baby's fingers
carrying the little angel in my arms
Was the first one
Happiness with emotions were never gone

When the second one appeared
Heart and Brain equally treasured
Well lucky was Bangalore
We missed her at Coimbatore
Such a bundle of treasure

Look at that wooden piece
The beautiful masterpiece
Being driven by my niece
That brown geometric piece

In your smile, I find my peace
In your touch, I feel the warmth
Keep glowing, Keep growing,
Keep smiling, Keep Shining,
The stars in my life,
They are my Love Doves
They are my Nieces!!!

Melancholy Travel

Walking down after the trek
A friend of mine did that click
The rock welcomed me with the moisture
That was just a perfect posture

Though my legs were aching
Yet I sat there smiling and cherishing
The walk, strangers being friends, all-around
teasing
Today I miss travelling
But I am not complaining

I am grateful for what I have
I will be always grateful for what I have
Healing the scars and pain
The memories of the train

First German Taste

Look at that grin
It was a trek in the woods around to reach and get
a glimpse
The White fairyland was not the Disneyland
Rocks and mountains that were hard
Amidst the beautiful white crystals land

No Beer No Wine
Yet did I Survive?
Shattered cold and nervous
Cheers with a blush

Draping Mom's colourful saree
Carrying Mom's cheerful smile
Well odd one out in this outfit
Curiosity in the foreigner's mind
Let this be the trend
On the foreign land
That was my last day
They told me should have worn every day

Romanian Friend

Shadows around the frame
Colourful memory in the glass

How I treasured the conversation
Before leaving the foreign country
Excited about coming to my home country
Beginning of our friendship story
Promising to continue our story

Talking about when we meet again
Dreaming together to travel again
Planning our future trips in 2019
Executing our trips in 2020
Still planning in 2021
Unknown about when is next

Even today counting on each other
Even today expressing our gratitude for each
other
Hoping to meet soon each other

Maa and Papa's Love

The love story of 1980
Sea of Feelings deeply
Ocean of Emotions intensely
Relationships were not a treaty

Communication was through letters
The postman was the delivery partner back then
The Swiggy or Zomato for love letters

They fought every single day
Keeping Egos at bay
Being there for each other
the support of a pillar
Untold yet Expressed
They didn't have to say
Loving each other more day by day

Maa ~ Mother

Mornings cherished, with caring scolds, from Dad,
Weekend lunch times, your place empty now,
Nights endless, gossips abound, emotions avow.

There is a void which
no one can fill and no words will heal, yet the
memories,
your teachings are carved in our hearts.

Teaching me to spread unconditionally
Love, Care and affection
Something I learnt from you
I was not there when you wanted me
You are not here when I write this.
Irony of life.

She made me believe in my core values
For every moment of joy and pampering I miss
you.
I miss your lap, your hugs and moments
where I can just talk talk talk my heart out or even
cry out.

For all that on the picture from earrings to the
several accessories
Reflecting on the Saree, it is a memory filled with
treasure which I preserve
I wish you were here and the only wish I would
ever wish
which can not be fulfilled...
For all I know in your layers of protection I will
never be shattered.
For the days when my heart breaks, when I fall
down,
I know your name, your picture,
your lessons will give me all that strength to
traverse through.

For the days when I am getting the blocks of my
dream achieved,
I know you will be proud.
For we have seen dreams together
You are the constant star in my galaxy of life who
makes sure I shine
Your memories are and will always be
My source of strength even in your absence

The Story of the Lone White Hibiscus

The infinite sky symbolizes
that is the place where sun rises and sun sets
like the ups and downs in our lives

I am growing every day with you.
As I water you with every droplet so does my
mind resonates every moment to calm down and
make peace with life.
Look forward go with the flow
Take things easy and slow
There are moments of blow
There are moments to glow.
Temporary is permanent in life
Still life goes on and on.

Marigold

I love oranges
I love orange colour
I love orange flower
Orange for me is so therapeutic
I remembered an old memory of an orange dress

The petals, the layers
The ornament for my letters in the future
The ornament for my terrace in the present

The tall building resembles the expectations
around
The sky shows the limitless possibilities.
And I stand there small yet beautiful
Oh my Marigold!
Just be bold!
As I was told
Some are cold
Some are warm
Some do no harm
So stay calm
The lines on my palm
Have the unexpressed story
Taking me to a destiny

Carving some hearts
Craving some desires
Making memories
Crossing the feeling of an ocean
Filled with mixed emotion
No justification
As life is just an exhibition!

Life is Beautiful

I have been healing myself
with scars for the last few days and months and
years
I am shattered I am broken
I smile and I cry
I eat and I fast
I have to admit that this phase is not easy
I study and I dream
I concentrate and I'm distracted
I focus and I diverge
Yet Life is beautiful
Life is all about hopes
Life is all about experiences

Privilege

A morning if you can smell a marigold
get your hands dirty with mud on the terrace
plants
remove the weeds
can walk can make tea for Dad
have breakfast with him
can hug Mom and kiss her
hear that love-bundled scolding
You have a privilege

I love to admit

I am shattered I am broken
I divert my attention to what I have
I divert my attention to what I want to achieve
I love to admit that I am fighting internally
I love to admit that I am not complaining anymore
I love to admit that I am dealing with losses
I love to admit that I am dealing with heartbreaks
I love to admit that I am shattered
I love to admit that I am tired
I love to admit that I am not okay
I love to admit that I need a break
I love to admit that I am a mixed tape of emotions
Lighten up my burden
Though life is beautiful it is not easy
Though life is challenging your presence is making it
easy
I love to admit that I need a shoulder
I love to admit that I am grateful
Because you are there to listen

Sweet Bitter Twenty-Five

Twenty-Five years in the cultural city
Twenty-Five years in the cotton city
Walking and holding hands in hand
Both of them grew their child

She craved to go beyond boundaries
Her sisters lived in different territories
She fought she complained
All went in vain and drained
Why things revolve in circles she wondered

On the verge of losing her mother
The woman she most loved
Nothing is more important than the one
We adore and care

Her world revolved around her
Her mother who always won
Just not hearts but
But made her father skip beats
With her beauty
And she never failed in her duties

January snow in Germany
May summers in Hospital beds
Life takes a U-turn
With the snap of fingers
Life changes are triggered

She saw her Dad
For the first time so sad
This time he was shattered
The pain was deep and hammered

No words to console
Losing a loved one
who was so dear
The loss of love immersed in tears
Grief is tough to bear

Twenty-five was hard
Life changed its card
Diverse emotions and battles on the thread
The women evolved and evolved

Papa ~ Father

I am lost yet trying to find myself
Being short of words
Shot on that afternoon
When you breathed last

I miss the morning voice filled with a smile
blessings for a lovely day
With your palms on my head

I don't have the afternoons to share my lunch
rants.
I don't have the evenings where we shared our
routine talks
I don't have nights where I would sit for dinner
together and pour my heart out.

There is a lot left to do but there was a lot done.
There is life ahead but there was a life before.
There was you, us and now?

Tears will roll down
but I don't have fatherly hands to wipe them off.
My heart is heavy but I don't have the fatherly hug
to make that light.

I will miss you Dad for every moment in my life
For all the sacrifices you and Mom did
for your daughters
even this life is going to be a debt that we would
owe you...

Your love, your words, your wisdom
Gives no vacuum of loneliness in my life
Your blessings will continue to grow
in addition to Mom's love and blessings for
eternity.

Your soul, always will love us,
care for us and protect us rest in peace.
Forever yours and only yours
The Beti who will always be proud of you!

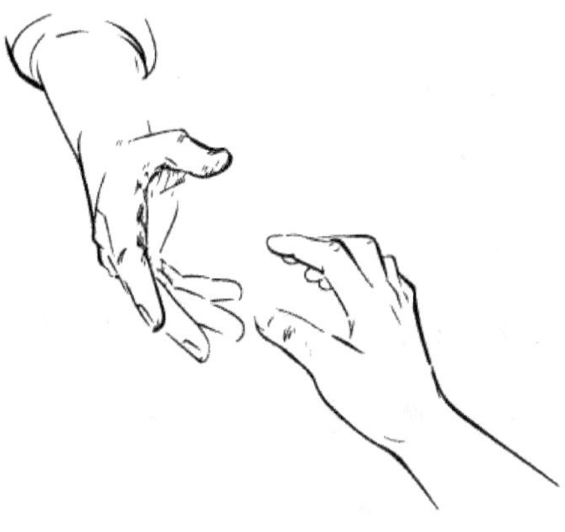

Letter to My Readers
of the Book

Dear Reader,

Greetings !!!

I hope that as you read this, the words in the book make you smile. Writing this book of poems has been a labor of love, and I am thankful to my family, and the incredible individuals who have touched my life along the way. This collection is a poetic journey of my life filled with crests and troughs of good and bad times. At one point in time, I did wish I had written this book when my parents were alive and I consoled myself by saying, "Being late is better than never",

which also was taught to me by my Dad.
Thank you to each and every one of you for
being a part of this poetic journey. Your
presence and support with you holding this
book and reading this have made this
endeavour truly meaningful. May these
poems bring joy, introspection, nostalgia
and beauty to all who read them.

With heartfelt thanks,
Charulatha Jain